Turtle T...

What Is a Turtle?

A turtle is a reptile.
So is a snake, a lizard,
and a crocodile.

Snake

Lizard

Crocodile

Did You Know?

All reptiles have cold blood. They feel cool when you touch them.

Always wash your hands after handling a turtle.

3

A turtle has a hard shell.
It has a hard beak.
It has no teeth.
It can see well.

shell

tail

eye

beak

mouth

tongue

neck

claws

foot

Did You Know?

A turtle can
pull itself
into its shell
just like
a snail does.

A turtle has
a pattern on its shell.
Its skin has
a pattern, too.

The pattern on
each turtle's shell
is different,
just like
people's fingerprints
are different.

7

A turtle lays eggs.
When the eggs hatch,
the babies have to look
after themselves.

Did You Know?

Baby turtles are food for lots of bigger animals.

Where Do Turtles Live?

Some turtles live
in ponds or streams.
Some turtles live in the sea.
Some turtles live on land.

Did You Know?

A tortoise
is also a turtle.
A tortoise
lives on land.

A turtle can stay
under the water
for a long time.
It comes up
for air.

Did You Know?

A turtle can be a good pet.

What Do Turtles Eat?

Some turtles eat
fruits and flowers and leaves.
Some turtles eat
worms and insects.
Some turtles eat fish.

Index